GOD SPEAKS TO WOMEN

STEPHANIE MCALISTER JENNINGS

Stephanie Jennings Ministries
Mitchellville, Maryland 20721

Published in the United States by
Stephanie Jennings Ministries
Mitchellville, Maryland

Library of Congress Cataloging-in-Publication Data
93-080372

Stephanie McAlister Jennings
God Speaks to Women

ISBN 0-9639396-0-2

Printed in the United States of America
Fourth Printing

Cover Photo by

Stanley Smith

Dedication

This work is dedicated to my mommy and in memory of my daddy who introduced me to my lord and Savior Jesus Christ.

Acknowledgements

"TO GOD BE THE GLORY FOR THE THINGS HE HAS DONE"

I thank God for my husband and my children who rolled with the punches and cooperated so willingly at the times that I needed their understanding the most.

I also praise the Lord for all of our friends and loved ones who offered encouragement, support, comments and constructive criticisms that aided in the refining of this work.

I am particularly grateful to Rev. Eugene Weathers, D.Min., for calling out the gift to write that was within me and to his wife Lisa for sharing a word from God which moved me toward the completion of this book.

Contents

Foreword

More than ever, the pressures of life demand the wisdom and guidance that are only offered in the Word of God. As family ties fade and the boundaries between acceptable and unacceptable social behavior become ever so faint, Christians struggle to make sense of the world as we know it.

When the painful lessons of everyday living are combined with the lessons of God's Word, real wisdom is born. The voice of this wisdom is that of the preacher.

In "God Speaks To Women" we hear a voice, neither shrill nor muffled. It is the voice of a wife, a mother, a preacher. Rev. Jennings speaks to today's Christians, those of us who seek to be hearers and doers of God's Word. This book sheds light on the practical application of the Word, brings a clearer understanding and inspires us toward a closer walk with Christ.

Lisa V. Weathers

Introduction

It is my desire that this writing will illuminate the thinking of women everywhere and get them to understand that God truly is no respecter of person. The title, <u>God Speaks To Women</u>, expresses the reality of His Omnipresence. For surely God has spoken to women in the past, is speaking to women now and will continue to speak to women in the future.

I pray that you will find this writing to be a blessing in your walk with God and that it will move you to desire to seek His Blessed Face even the more.

Stephanie M. Jennings

CHAPTER ONE

CONQUERING YOURSELF

"Nay, in all these things we are more than conquerors through him that loved us."

(Romans 8:37)

As maturing believers, we steadfastly concern ourselves with the issue of victorious living. We feel our greatest challenge is to overcome the "wiles of Satan." Grant it, he has proved himself a worthy opponent--one not to be taken lightly. Nevertheless, we must realize that a task set before us supersedes conquering Satan--conquering our "Self."

"And having in a readiness to revenge all disobedience, when your obedience is fulfilled," (II Corinthians 10:6).

Paul, in his letter to the Romans writes, "For to be carnally minded is death; but to be spiritually minded is life and peace" (Romans 8:6). Notice, he has given us two dimensions of being spiritually minded--life and peace. Life has two facets--present and eternal. The Gospel of John records that Jesus told the disciples, "The thief cometh not, but for to steal, and to kill and to destroy: I am come that they might have life, and that they might have it more abundantly."

A number of verses in God's Word reveal His divine plan for a life on earth full of health, prosperity, and abundance for his people. We must, however, take three steps to benefit from this plan. First, we must believe it is God's Will for us to prosper. Many of our blessings are not seen, and our dreams and hopes unrealized because Satan robs us by planting in our hearts the lie that the wealthy and prosperous are wicked and hell bound. Bah! Humbug!

"Beloved, I wish above all things that thou mayest prosper and be in health, even as thy soul prospereth" (III John v. 2).

God's word very clearly draws a parallel between salvation and abundant, victorious living, a benefit to which we are entitled.

Second, we must know that God can perform His Will. It is one thing to will or to desire something for someone, but another thing to bring it to pass. God is more than capable. He is omnipotent or "almighty." The potential and capabilities of all others are fragments, minute parts of His omnipotence. Paul stated it nicely when he said, "For in Him we live, and move, and have our being" (Acts 17:28). Not only are we found in Him, but "everything was made by Him; and without Him was not anything made that was made" (John. 1:3). Even Satan has no power of himself. He too uses the power granted to him by God. "The Lord made all things for himself; yea, even the wicked for the day of evil" (Proverbs 16:4). To allow Satan to rob us is shameful. He too depends on our God for his substance. Our heavenly Father is the enemy's source of existence and the provider of his power. He can only oppose us with God's permission. He can only afflict us with what we will accept. We must learn to tell Satan, "NO!" We now have authority over him through the blood of Jesus Christ.

Third, we must desire, or we must will, to live victoriously. The first step is ours. Jehovah is the covenant God. Having entered into covenant with Him, we are now fellow yokemen, partners with God. We are not to be spiritual invalids, leaving all of the work to Him; we are laborers with Him. We are His servants. To many Christians, salvation means God serving them, waiting on them and ministering to them—but we are his servants. We are to bless His Name, serving Him with gladness. Too often we take the term "wait" to mean sitting and resting. But to truly "wait" on God is to serve Him while we believe Him to perform His Word. For example, when we go to a restaurant, a waiter or waitress serves us in the good faith that we will pay what is right. Because we are not invalids, but endowed and empowered we can now move from within ourselves to embrace what God has provided for us.

The second aspect to life is eternal life. "For

God so loved the world, that He gave His only begotten Son, that whosoever believeth in Him should not perish but have everlasting life" (John 3:16). For many of us, this scripture was the first we memorized and, probably, the first one we taught our children. I believe we have failed to see the true blessing in this verse. It unveils the depth and degree of God's love for us in that He gave His son so that we, unworthy, ungrateful, and unable to meet His standards, could be reconciled to Him that He may share His Glory with us. Again, Paul says to be spiritually minded is life and peace. I am convinced that once we overcome the mind of our flesh and seek the mind of God, we are released from the agony of our constant struggle and inner conflict between our will and God's Will for us. Yes, the flesh wars against the Spirit, and the Spirit wars against the flesh; therefore, our complete surrender tips the scale in God's favor. The result is an internal calmness and confidence that the Master of the sea is not only on board the ship, but also at the helm, controlling the elements of our circumstances and situations.

"Because the carnal mind is enmity against God" (Romans 8:7). The mind of the flesh is no doubt one of the culprits with which we wrestle that Paul speaks of in Ephesians 6. Second Corinthians (10:4-5) addresses this issue more precisely and in bolder terms: "For the weapons of our warfare are not carnal, but mighty through God to the pulling down of strongholds; casting down imaginations, and every high thing that exalteth itself against the knowledge of God, and bringing into captivity every thought to the obedience of Christ."

The fifth verse speaks of casting down imaginations and bringing into captivity every thought to the obedience of Christ. Now to whose imaginations and thoughts do you suppose Paul was referring? Why ours, of course. For he urges us in the next verse to have in readiness to revenge all disobedience, when our obedience is fulfilled. Isn't that something! We are admonished to go forth as conquerors of God's enemy once we have conquered our "Self." When we are carnal minded (or self- motivated), we concern ourselves with matters of the flesh and the things of this world. We strive for material gain rather than the riches of God's glory. Walking in a carnal mind channels our energies and directs our focus away from Him who made us for His pleasure. This is why we find ourselves "searching for God" and "looking for a Word" when God is present and the Word has been given. It is the carnal-minded Christians who believe that God has left them or express feelings of spiritual inadequacy for truly they have fallen short of the greatest commandment--to love God with all thine heart, soul, mind, and strength.

Why is a spiritual mind a prerequisite to peace? When we can walk through this physical world and look (depart) neither to the right nor to the left, we walk victoriously. To have peace from fleshly desires is total deliverance from one's "self," and the ultimate level of maturity in a believer. Do not misinterpret what I am saying. We shall always be tempted. But as we mature, choosing God's Will becomes less stressful and more satisfying. We know it is out of lust that sin is brought forth. Our fleshly lusts and desires create a driving force in us-- a current more compelling than any other entity known to man. Turning our minds to satisfy the "self," subsequently turns our hearts away from God, inevitably taking us away from God's Will. We must realize that the path of the flesh and the path of the Spirit are not parallel, but opposing. Romans (8:8) tells us that flesh cannot please God. It is the mind of Christ that we must possess and His Spirit we must follow.

As we realize the need to conquer our "self," we must recognize what it is we must overcome. First, we must conquer our fleshly desires. As stated previously in this chapter, we stand at life's crossroads daily, having to choose the way of life or the way of death ("for the wages of sin is death"). As we examine the dimensions of fleshly desire, we must realize that we should consider many aspects.

For when we speak of "fleshly desires or lust," we know that there are several dimensions like (1) a longing for material wealth and social status; (2) a need for personal fulfillment by receiving approval, acceptance, and respect from others; (3) an uncontrollable hunger for power and control; and (4) a yearning for physical satisfaction--sexual gratification, overindulgence of food, substances, excessive spending, etc.

The carnal-minded believer cannot find rest in God or peace because of the insatiable need to fulfill these desires. This obsession, with satisfying the "self," consumes the individual and leads to a superficial and unproductive Christian life. Not only are we rendered unfruitful, but also we can often be found in financial devastation from this uncontrollable dilemma.

"Dearly beloved, I beseech you as strangers and pilgrims, abstain from fleshly lusts, which war against the soul" (I Peter 2:11).

Frequently, we fall to our knees and place the burden of our fleshly mortification in God's hands. We must know that we alone bear responsibility for possessing our vessels in sanctification and honor, laying aside every weight and the sin that does so easily beset us. It is up to each of us to identify the weak areas of our lives and to exercise the discipline necessary to overcome these pitfalls. As a defense mechanism, many of us choose to blame others and circumstances, past and present, for our lack of "God Control." However, if we are to be true overcomers, we must face the realities of life and set our goals toward perfection in the Spirit. It grieves me to see so many professing Christians complacent and comfortable in their salvation. "God has not told me to move so I must be all right," they say. Or, "Every time I make an effort the doors are shut, so it must not be God's Will." Usually when I inquire, these words spring forth from believers who, admittedly, have deficient prayer lives and who never fast. Of course, the doors are shut. Not because God wills them so but because the enemy has set a stronghold there to block the path. Conquering one's "self" means taking authority over a lackadaisical approach to God's business. We must shake the shackles of satisfaction with our marginal lifestyles and seek to soar like eagles to the highest heights of excellence in Him who loves us.

Overcoming our "self" is the ultimate test of our faith in God's hand of deliverance. For now we must believe Him beyond the point of faith unto salvation into a level of obedience. Obedience is an act of faith in God's Word. It says, "I trust you to fulfill your promises to me and through me." For God calls us to be vessels and instruments that He may use to bless his people. Because we believe Him and His Word, we are now able to say, "I give my "self" to you. I give you my goals and objectives; my hopes and dreams; my desires and wants. And if they are not what you have for me, I freely yield to your will. If I say mansion and You say, 'Hut.' Okay. If I say law school and You say 'No.' So be it. If I say Mercedes and You say, 'Bus.' I yield.!"

Yielding to God's Will is not always a sin issue. Yielding to God for many, if not all of us, may entail starting new lives. It may mean ending careers we have struggled all our lives to build, or it may mean discarding degrees we have worked hard to earn. Because all things work together for our good, these elements of our lives that we must sacrifice now are not wasted; however, God has placed them on the back burner of our lives to be used later as tools of our ministry.

Over and over again, I hear supposed Christians complaining of being in a "hard place," a place of hardship, despair, a barren land. There are times when God calls us to an uncomfortable, unfamiliar, and unanticipated path. When we don't understand His purpose or His logic and defy Him and rebel against Him by refusing to yield to Him, we may well find ourselves in this "hard place." When this is the case, we blame God by saying it is His Will that we are not flourishing, or it is His Will that we are in pain. We belong to Him. We must stop struggling to become what we want to be when we "grow up" and surrender to the skillful hands of the potter. For I declare unto you, we cannot "arrive" until we yield ourselves to God's Will and do it His Way. Forsake your dreams and follow the vision He has for your life. Remember, "where He leads, He feeds and where He guides, He provides." If you are in a barren land, more than likely you are not standing in the flow of His Will, for the Holy Spirit makes things happen. To launch out into the deep, the believer must realize that to mortify the flesh--or one's "self"—is no longer an option but a necessity.

"If ye then be risen with Christ seek those things which are above, where Christ sitteth on the right hand of God. Set your affection on things above, not on things on the earth. For ye are dead, and your life is hid with Christ in God. When Christ, who is our life, shall appear, then shall ye also appear with him in glory" (Colossians 3:1-4).

We are responsible for the souls of those yet wandering in darkness and lost in sin. To complete our endless task of soul winning, we must be well-trained, finely tuned instruments of God. This level of operation comes only through self-denial and obedience.

"And having in a readiness to revenge all disobedience, when your obedience is fulfilled" (II Corinthians 10:6).

Having established the need to conquer our fleshly desires, we must turn our attention to the emotional "self." Our emotions act as thermostats—dictating our interpretations of and responses to situations and people with whom we interact.

God's Word tells us that the enemy comes but to steal, kill and destroy. Satan uses our emotions to manipulate us toward unrighteous behavior. Through his lies and masterful deception, he creates in us an unacceptable emotional state. If he can convince us that we are lonely, depressed, unhappy, inferior, inadequate, etc., we eventually manifest these feelings in our Christian walk and will inevitably live defeated lives. We can counteract these attacks by first recognizing that the cause of our behavior is our feelings and, subsequently, set out to medicate our emotional "self" with the healing power of God's Word. Remember, identifying the problem is not enough. We must take our medicine to be made whole.

Because the emotional "self" is so overwhelming when it is rendered dysfunctional, we must be mindful to arrest any disorders immediately. Truly, the joy of the Lord is our strength, and that strength is susceptible only to emotional turmoil. For it is through our emotions that Satan robs us of our joy.

I dare not leave this topic without turning your attention toward the devastating effects of guilt. This mind set is so destructive because it is debilitating. No other emotion tears at the fabric of our faith as strongly as guilt. Satan lures us into the deep, murky waters of guilt only to leave us to sink to the depths with the weights of self-pity, shame, self-hatred, and hopelessness chained around our necks. In such moments of despair, we must take hold of God's Word, believing nothing can separate us from His love.

Finally, we must conquer our fearful "self." Fear is more crippling than any disease that has ever invaded the human body. Once fallen victim to fear we cannot reign victoriously. So overwhelming is its effects in the life of man that John left on record in Revelations (21:8) that the fearful would have their part in the lake of fire, the second death.

Why would a God of mercy condemn those faint of heart to eternal damnation? John 15:1-8 gives us further insight for life in Christ.

"I am the true vine, and my father is the husbandman. Every branch in me that beareth not fruit he taketh away . . ."

Our primary function as Christians is to glorify God. Here John reveals that all unfruitful branches will be gathered and cast into the fire. Fear prohibits healthy development and maturation of believers, stunting growth and thereby rendering one unfruitful. Fear promotes stagnation and creates hindrances in the life of God's people. Far too often, believers tell me that they are not going forth to do what God has commanded them because of fearful inhibitions. We care for our loved ones, but we must not allow them to hinder us. It is intimidating to accept new challenges, but in Christ we know we are overcomers.

"For God hath not given us the spirit of fear; but of power, and of love, and of a sound mind" (II Timothy 1:7).

"There is no fear in love; but perfect love casteth out fear; because fear hath torment. He that feareth is not made perfect in love" (I John 4:18).

We must always be aware of the symptoms of fear in our walk. Procrastination, abnormal feelings of insecurity, reluctance to take advantage of opportunities, and failure to move forward into new ventures are signals of the abiding spirit of fear hiding in the dark corners of our minds. Because Satan is a counterfeiter, he attempts to mask fear behind the disguise of "wisdom" by raising the question of God's Will for our lives. Often, his voice can be heard in the recesses of our minds whispering, "Is this God's Will for you? Are you stepping ahead of God?" And if we are not careful, we will succumb to this farce by finding ourselves at a stand still as we "wait on the Lord."

Because we know that our lives are not our own, we must acknowledge that others are affected by what happens in our lives. If we are rendered inept because we have allowed fear to grip us and take hold of the reins of our minds, we become instrumental in creating an avalanche into the lives of those around us who, sometimes unknowingly, trust and depend on us for spiritual motivation, guidance, and intercession on their behalf, for we must bear the infirmities of the weak. We are responsible as soldiers of the cross for overcoming our fears.

Up to this point, we have discussed the necessity for conquering our fleshly desires, emotions, and fears to glorify God, edify the body of Christ, and personify the ultimate goal of the believer--spiritual maturity in every area of our lives. Now we must ask ourselves, "What tools do I use to aid in this trying but enriching quest of conquering my "self"? The answer is quite simply--fasting, praying, and feasting on God's Word. According to the words of Jesus, some deliverances take place only as a result of these mechanisms (Matthew 17:21).

Now you may say, "There's nothing new in these techniques." This is true, for they are the principle factors in Christian growth and demonstration of God's power in the lives of believers. However, another factor works with these three and brings them to life—obedience.

In discussing fleshly desires, I listed those things that stimulate the body like food, sex, narcotics, greed, and power. We must always be aware that there is a "mind" of the flesh that lurks in every secret place of man's heart waiting for an opportunity to corrupt. It is this mind that rises against us as we walk after or follow the "mind" of the Spirit. And it is the voice of the fleshly mind that cries out to us in an attempt to turn our wills away from God. It is by fasting that we quiet this voice, for fasting breaks the will of the flesh and places it under subjection to God's Will.

Through prayer, we enter the mind of God to know His Will. Through His written Word, he confirms His Will for us as members of the Body of Christ and soldiers of the cross.

When Jesus told the Pharisees they swallow a camel and gag at a gnat, he was trying to get them to realize that they were overlooking the obvious in their attempt to discern the "mysteries" of God. Such is the case with some modern believers. In their attempts to be deep in the Lord, they miss God.

In our daily task to fulfill God's Will for our lives, in our day-to-day struggle to do His good pleasure, and our ongoing attempt to "whip the devil," we don't grasp the truths of God most relevant to our spiritual walk. Many times I hear believers speak of the rigors of life and its interference with their ability to be overcomers and walk victoriously. It is always, "I don't have time" or "I have to do so much, even "I need to think about so many other things." God challenges us to conquer "self" first. In so doing, we minimize distractions. For if we truly desire to reflect the ageless words of Paul, "Nay in all these things we are more than conquerors through Him that loved us" (Romans 8:37), we must first conquer our "self."

CHAPTER TWO

HORMONES AND THE HOLY SPIRIT

The issue of hormones is crucial to the life of every woman because of the effects they have on many of our lives. However, God has shown us through His Word that even though this phenomenon is very real we are more than conquerors. We can reign victoriously over hormones through the Holy Spirit. Therefore, it is essential that we establish certain truths which are our ground to stand on.

"Finally my brethren, be strong in the Lord, and in the power of his might. Put on the whole armour of God, that ye may be able to stand against the wiles of the devil (Ephesians 6:10-11).

The first truth is that Satan has a plan for our lives. Be sure to know that just as God has a plan or a will for our lives--Satan does also. When reading this scripture, most believers focus on the whole armour of God. But we cannot begin to address the putting on of the armour of God until we take a closer and serious look at the wiles of Satan. For some reason we tend to brush over that word, it escapes our concern. The word wiles is translated from the Greek word, methodia. So we are actually talking about the methods of Satan: the strategies, techniques, and tactics of his master plan. We can no longer afford to look at small pieces of the picture. This means we must move from believing the devil is spending his time tampering with our cars and hiding our keys and begin to search for the whole picture which is, he desires to steal our souls.

To that end, he has devised a master plan for our lives and has ordered his imps and demons to execute it at any cost. To defeat his purpose, we must learn the mind of the enemy. When athletes train, they study their opponents' techniques and playing strategies. Chess players learn to move their pieces with precision based on calculations of three probable responses by their opponents. No chess piece is sacrificed for nought. Likewise, we must be mindful that Satan never brings anything our way as an isolated incident. There is a reason for everything that opposes us. Satan plays for keeps. Our spiritual ruin is all that he is concerned with—not spills on our dresses or runs in our stockings.

Therefore, we are aware that Satan has contempt for our joy. He will do whatever is necessary to rob us of it, for the joy of the Lord is our strength. It is the strength of our faith. Without faith, we cannot

please God; without faith, we cannot move moun-
tains; without faith, we cannot speak things that are
not as though they were, and they come into being;
without faith, we cannot be healed; without faith, we
cannot live victoriously. Satan comes to steal our
inheritance and all that God has willed for us. He
comes to rob us of our health; he comes to rob us of
our prosperity. God says I will give you favor in the
eyes of men. Nevertheless, Satan will come against
us and will try to interfere with our benefits and our
prosperity. Now we know that prosperity is not
always financial. We can prosper emotionally, for
God can give us peace in the midst of a storm, and,
subsequently, we will prosper in health. Our skins
will take on a new glow. Our hair will shine and
grow. Even our wombs can become fruitful. But
we must know that Satan can only steal our joy by
touching our emotions, not by touching our finances
or our health or possessions. For it is not these
factors that constitute the level of our joy but the way
we are affected by situations and circumstances in-
volving them. When our joy is full, no mountain is
insurmountable, no river is uncrossable, no cross is
too heavy. When our joy is full our attitude is
Hallelujah anyhow!

Next he wants to kill our testimony because of
its power over his works. "And they overcame him
by the blood of the Lamb and by the word of their
testimony" (Revelations 12:11). Satan will tempt us
to fall so our testimonies will make us appear as

liars, hypocrites, and fools. If we claim God a healer, Satan will attempt to place upon you the symptoms of disease. If we stand declaring deliverance and victory in a certain area of our lives, Satan will set about to make us an open shame and target of ridicule. Satan will do everything in his power to invalidate our testimonies.

Finally, Satan wants to destroy our faith in God. Once we lose our confidence; once we lose our faith; once we no longer know, that we know in whom we have believed, doubt creeps in and fear comes forth. At this point, God's hands become tied in our lives not because He's no longer able, but because we cannot receive what He has for us. Many times we miss our blessings or hinder them, I should say, because we do not believe God enough to look to Him for our needs and hearts' desires.

I am attempting to express to you the importance of seriously considering this issue of hormones and the Holy Spirit. It is a matter of urgency because under the disguise of hormonal imbalances, Satan grips us without resistance. God spoke to me in a women's fellowship as I was preparing to teach on this subject and commanded me to declare that there is a difference between our experiencing a human hormonal process and being attacked by Satan with the "Spirit of. . . ." Let me make myself clear. God has created us to have monthly cycles in which our hormonal levels are altered. However, Satan camouflages his demonic spirits in the cycle by allowing them to manifest only during certain scheduled and anticipated times. For instance, if we willingly receive depression in our lives three days out of the month based on the theory of Pre-Menstrual Syndrome (PMS), Satan can afflict us with the spirit of depression which will only manifest at that time. Now, that we are open to accept it, the spirit of depression can encompass us and subtly manipulate us during the rest of the month. The danger in this is that Satan sends his spirits in groups. For instance, where there's jealousy, we are sure to find insecurity. Anger, hatred, and murder usually accompany one another, and fear and anxiety run together. So I'm saying, chances are if we accept one demonic influence, we can look forward to being introduced to many more. I say influenced because Satan cannot possess those filled with the Holy Spirit, but he can oppress them. However, if we are not washed in the blood of the Lamb and filled with His Spirit we are candidates for demonic possession.

Satan is cunning. If he knows that he cannot attack us overtly or plant his demonic spirits around us, and we receive them willingly; it is not beneath him to cloak himself as a messenger of God or to package his gift of death to imitate a gift from God. Some of us are weak and carnal minded, so he can entice us. However, those of us who are mature and discerning must be approached from a different angle. That angle, I would dare say is PMS or "the spirit of PMS."

Careful observation of the behavioral patterns of those who accept the PMS theory will prove it true that the movement of this spirit begins to manifest itself increasingly beyond its initial time frame and invades during other times of the month. Inevitably, all unsavory behavior and irrational responses are explained away as PMS and occur more frequently. Many who once found themselves depressed on the first, second, and third of the month, now struggle with depression the entire month.

As I said before, each of us has a different level of vulnerability. Some of us who are immature are more susceptible to small attacks and quick defeats. Because of this fact, I take issue with my Christian sisters. It seems as though many of us allow trivial matters to deter us from reaching our potential in God. When I ask my sisters why they are not putting forth a greater effort to make themselves available to be used mightily by the Lord, I hear everything from "My children need me with them twenty-four hours a day" to "My pastor told me I couldn't do (what God had commanded) it." Satan knows we are lazy and use our womanhood as an excuse. Oh yes, we can play the noble, self-sacrificing mother and the faithful, devoted wife, but God knows it is an escape mechanism, and we will have to give an account. Satan, likewise, is aware of our levels of faith and commitment. He is always searching for ways to cause us to stumble and land in his web of complacency. Unfortunately for some of us, he has found

PMS the most effective way to place us under arrest and to put our spiritual progress on hold. Once he can permeate our lives with depression, we become entrapped by a world of darkness, not knowing how to rebuke it in Jesus's name. But because it is camouflaged within our expectation and acceptance, it engulfs us and places an iron grip on our lives. We lose pride in our appearance; social activities and fellowship with our loved ones are not important; and we are not stimulated and consequently we lose our love for life. We say it is PMS. But, God tells us to be aware of the spirit of depression.

Depression, psychologists say, is "frozen rage," a neurotic response. It is anger turned inward. Because many of us are unaggressive and unable to verbalize our feelings of resentment and violation, we turn our anger inward. We displace our feelings by internalizing them and they manifest as depression. Although depression is an explainable biological process, we must realize that there is a "spirit of depression." If we accept the theory of PMS and the symptoms of PMS, we leave ourselves open to receive the "spirit of depression" that will mask itself as a PMS symptom. This spirit will slowly mold our character and become embedded in our personalities. Inevitably, we will flow with its pattern. The spirit of depression will soon manifest its presence in our lives, for there is no way to avoid being altered by what we endure.

Before the Lord healed me from spinal arthritis, my doctor noted that my back had become distorted to the point it was no longer symmetrical. She explained that such was the case because I had subconsciously maneuvered my body to avoid the points of pain. Similarly, when we are in spiritual distress, we can only hide the evidence for a short time before it is manifested.

How do we avoid becoming distorted by Satan's attack upon us with PMS? The same way we stand against all of his wiles. By doing what renders us sensitive to the Holy Spirit—fasting, prayer, and searching God's Will and His Way through His Word. As we mature in Christ, our discernment becomes keener. We no longer take for granted every incident, situation, and circumstance. We must be determined to bind Satan on every side and to identify and pull down his strongholds wherever they are set up in our lives.

Satan intends to render us ineffective as witnesses for Christ. For in so doing, not only are we stunted, but he does not need to be concerned with God using us as instruments of deliverance in another's life. Our job description as Christians is to glorify God. And when we fail to do so, we fail God.

You may ask, "What difference does it make if I lose control of myself a couple of days a month? Surely, it can't really be of great importance." Surely it can! First and foremost, it disrupts our interpersonal relationships. So often, in a moment of hormonal haphazardness, we speak or do irreparable harm to a loved one or friend. The unpredictable, erratic behavior of those who boast of suffering from PMS has shaken and all but destroyed more than a few marriages. Many times, I have listened to distraught husbands declare how confused they were by their wives' volatile temperaments. One brother said that he did not indulge his wife as he would like because he did not know from one moment to the next how she would accept his attempts to show his feelings, so he did nothing.

Because women set the tone or the mood for the home, we must always be aware of what we are transferring to the children. A stressed out, frantic mother produces stressed out, frantic children. When my husband comes in out of sorts, the children don't notice as long as I don't react. No one panics until Mamma panics. If PMS is your thing, make sure it doesn't become your children's.

Our next concern should be the effect PMS has on our witness and testimonies as Christians. On our jobs, for instance, there are those who look to us to uphold the banner of the Lord. Our volatile behavior causes unbelievers distress when they can see no difference between our responses and their own. Many times the ungodly look to us to stabilize the environment. They are secure in knowing our God hears and answers prayer. Although they cannot communicate with the Master, they trust God in us. What may seem an insignificant moment to you can destroy their confidence and faith in the transforming power of the Holy Spirit. One day of PMS responses can do considerable damage to one seeking God.

Furthermore, we find ourselves bound and held captive by the spirits we have allowed in our lives and so willingly accepted as symptoms of PMS. Because of this, we speak defeat. We speak against God in our lives.

How do we speak against God? We know that the words we speak become flesh or go forth and actualize. When we speak depression, sickness, fear, anger, etc., they go before us and block our paths. Whereas if we speak victory, faith, and trust in the Father and if we speak of Him as the Healer and Provider that He is, we release His Will in our lives. That Will is victorious over PMS and other bondages.

Many times we do not realize we are speaking against God. His Word tells us that anything not of faith is sin, including the words from our mouths. For as soon as they leave our lips, they fall into the hands of God's angels or Satan's imps. How busy has Satan been in your life lately? Maybe it is because your words have given him license to come against you.

The Word of God tells us that through all of Job's afflictions, he did not sin against God with his mouth. Very often, the Lord has released our blessings and opened doors for us, but because of a lack of faith, we speak against what He has done and miss

God or delay His hand from working on our behalves.

For example, how many times have we desired God to do something for us such as bless us with a new job or a promotion, maybe a house, car or some other need or desire; and as we proceeded to seek after these things we spoke doubt. Such as "I really don't know if God is going to do this for me" rather than "I believe God is able to perform it," and go forth in His Name.

Yes, we have been redeemed by the Blood of the Lamb. But until we learn to stop speaking against God in our daily lives, we still live in bondage and need deliverance. By no means are we to deny our womanhood. We must, however, be aware of the wiles of Satan. Please remember, we can do all things and be all things through Christ who strengthens us.

CHAPTER THREE

THE IMAGE OF GOD'S WOMAN

"And God said, Let us make man in our image, after our likeness: and let them have dominion over the fish of the sea, and over the fowl of the air, and over the cattle, and over all the earth, and over every creeping thing that creepeth upon the earth. So God created man in his own image, in the image of God created he him; male and female created he them. And God blessed them, and God said unto them, Be fruitful, and multiply, and replenish the earth, and subdue it: and have dominion over the fish of the sea, and over the fowl of the air, and over every living thing that moveth upon the earth" (Gen. 1:26-28).

We must first establish the difference between being God's woman and being a Christian woman. Sociologists tell us that a woman's referring to herself as a Christian may be based on several factors: (a) the religion of her family; (b) the religion of the church she attends; (c) the religion of her geographic location; (d) the religion of her ethnic group; or most important, (e) the religion whose tenets she practices. The latter is the case with the woman of God. God's woman is the woman who has allowed her life to show forth the manifestation of His Holy Spirit.

It is typical of today's society to esteem the value of a woman by the status of the man with whom she is associated. Because of that, we sometimes become devoted to the development and cultivation of our husbands or seek husbands who fit socially accepted profiles, instead of investing in ourselves and striving to reach the heights of our potential.

We have all fallen victim to the arrogant woman who boasts of the accomplishments of her spouse and is apparently consumed in his world. However, when she stands before the mirror to measure her self-worth based on the merits of her own life, she finds herself lacking. The tragedy of depending on someone else to validate our existence is that at any given moment that person may step off the stage of our lives. We are women whom God has chosen or taken unto himself. His status supersedes that of the most famous actors, the most renowned world leaders, the most acclaimed scientists, the most prestigious attorneys, or any men this world highly esteems.

The role of the man in the life of the woman is

to provide for her and to protect her. I believe that much can be determined about a man's character by observing his woman. If a brother is not fulfilling his financial obligations, not only does the wife suffer but also the children, for the woman is pulled out of the home to compensate for her spouse's deficiency. Likewise, when she is abused or neglected, what is happening internally will manifest in other areas of her life. However, when we see ourselves as God's women, we know we are provided for and protected by the ultimate source.

Now that we have determined ourselves to be God's women and not just Christian women, we must focus on the three images always present with us--the image that others have of us, the image we have of ourselves, and the image God has of us. We must accept that we are somewhat responsible for how others feel about us. We may feel that we are not responsible for the image others have of us. That it is their problem if they don't like us, don't understand us, or have misinterpreted us. If we look at ourselves objectively, we would no doubt discover certain factors that may establish the basis for conclusions others make about our lives. For instance, the manner in which we carry ourselves, the clothes we wear, or the "mask" we wear when we leave our homes and step on the stage of life contribute to the way others view us.

Many times I am approached by women concerned because regardless of how powerful they are in God or how mightily He uses them, they are not taken seriously in their ministries or professions. Ninety percent of the time, these women project themselves as women who can be had. Their dress is seductive and inappropriate for holy women, their walks are suggestive, and their postures with men are usually alluring. Although the brothers may find their company gracious, they do not view them as chosen vessels of the Lord.

All things are lawful, but not all things are expedient. Although we have liberty in the Spirit, we must come to terms with the fact that everyone is not free. Therefore, we can become stumbling blocks to those who have not reached our level of maturity. For example, the book of Corinthians addresses the argument whether Christians should eat meat sacrificed to idols. Paul realized that there was no other God but Jehovah and understood the brotherhood's taking advantage of the fact that only the best animals were sacrificed. However, he had to reprimand them for causing the babes in Christ offense because they were unable to accept their freedom in Jesus. Subsequently, he said that if eating meat offends your brother, don't eat meat.

There is schism in the Body of Christ today in that some say women should not wear slacks, and others say that wearing slacks is okay. God's Word instructs us to obey those who have rule over us. If your shepherd stands on Deuteronomy 22:5, then to disobey him brings you into transgression. It is not a matter of whether he's right or wrong; it is a matter of obedience. Too often I hear of situations in which women oppose the leaders of their local churches. The pastors are God's property, and it is up to Him to set things in order, not us. If we cannot submit to authority, we need to find another pastor. Of course, this is provided we are standing on the Word of God and not misinterpreting scripture ourselves.

There is one point I would like to make to the sisters who walk in liberty regarding slacks. Sometimes we need to use wisdom in determining what we put on our bodies based on our body structures. Slacks are not enhancing to certain figures. There's no need to boast of being delivered from wearing slacks if your dresses are "sprayed on," or, as one of my women associates says, "It is fittin'."

On the same note, my sisters, Satan is a liar. Looking like a hag does not connote righteousness. Many women would submit their lives to God if the myth would be dispelled that God's women are unkept, plain Janes who do nothing but fry chicken and have babies.

Several components may comprise the second image--the image we have of ourselves. Because of my work in women's ministry, I know how badly God's women need healing. The number of emotionally and psychologically damaged women in the Body is overwhelming. I am concerned about the need for deliverance in these areas because even in attempting to do our best, if we are not whole, if we

For our marriages to be successful, we must accept the truth about our situations and build on a realistic foundation. Although we may not be married to Don Juans, I am sure the qualities which attracted us to our husbands are still there. It is not fair to them or us to expect them to move out of their characters and become who we want them to be this week and next week or the week after that, depending on our mood swings.

Much of our hostility toward our spouses develops because they do not fulfill the romantic expectations we long for. But that was the sacrifice we made when we chose country boys with high school educations who haven't the slightest inkling of who Robert Browning was. So when they come in, pat us on the bottom, and say "What's for dinner?" or "Fix me a 'sammich,'" we get ticked off! Let's be real. We can hardly expect them to break forth in prose of love and devotion when they may have barely made it out of English 101.

In many cases, our sisters are single needlessly. Because society says "Mr. Right" must be tall, dark, and handsome; carry a briefcase; and wear suits to work, we overlook the construction workers and auto mechanics as marriage candidates. However, these men can make a buck whether the pay check stops or not. They are not only good on the job but also handy around the house. Some of us have husband material repairing our cars and kitchen sinks but don't see them for the treasures they are because of our delusions of grandeur, our unrealistic expectations.

The next factor that lends to the psychological component of our self-image is false information. In Genesis 3:5, Satan says, "For God doth know that in the day ye eat thereof, then your eyes shall be opened, and ye shall be as gods, knowing good and evil." Satan has some of us searching for what we already have. In his dialogue with Eve, Satan convinced her that she did not have all she needed when God had provided everything she could want or need, including her being like Him made in His very image and likeness.

When God calls us unto Himself, he endows us with gifts by His Spirit and gives us privilege to his treasure chest. All that he requires of us can be achieved because He extends to us His potential, His possessions, and His promises. He fulfills all our needs to satisfy His criteria or expectations of us as His women. Seeing ourselves as His women, we now realize that we must shed some things to conform more to the image of His Son.

If we look at the Samaritan woman who met Jesus at the well, we see Him impart upon her several new perspectives. First, He gave her a new perspective on men. She was accustomed, no doubt, to being the giver; to being the one who sacrificed to get the relationship to work, and to keeping everything intact. We know how it is, for even today women are still the givers. Some of us have to work, take care of ourselves, the children, and the men in our lives in addition to seeing that matters of the house are kept in order. But Jesus clarified his position by declaring, "If thou knewest the gift of God, and who it is that saith to thee, Give me to drink; thou wouldest have asked of him, and he would have given thee living water" (John 4:10). He spoke words to her that she was unaccustomed to hearing from a man -- "I will give to you."

Next, He gave her a new perspective on her "self." He forced her to see that she was a wretch undone. Although we may fancy ourselves women of sophistication and class, God's Holy Spirit exposes our pitiful state over and over again. Seeing pass our fine outer garments, looking pass our painted and perfumed exterior, Jesus sees our conditions and, as He did for the Samaritan woman, He offers us restoration; forcing us to confess, "I have no husband."

Even today, we have Christian sisters who, as the Samaritan woman did, have a prostitute's mentality-- offering ourselves to the highest bidder; marrying to obtain material wealth; marrying for convenience, prestige, and security. I am sadden to know that some women in God's house are marrying only to justify their whoredom. If we check their record we will find their lives to be one shack-up after another and still the one they have is not theirs. Jesus did not cover the Samaritan woman's whoredom, He cured it. We too can be cured, and with a new perspective of ourselves, we can tell others, "I have found a real man!" His name is Jesus.

Finally, He gave her a new perspective on her religious beliefs. In an attempt to manipulate the conversation, the woman raised the issue of the Holy Place. Jesus enlightened her by proclaiming, "God is Spirit: and they that worship Him must worship Him in spirit and in truth." So often we get hung up on what local church we attend, who the pastor is, and what social status the people who fellowship there have and we lose sight of the church's purpose—to seek and to save that which is lost. So Jesus stripped her of all that she held, leaving her to face the shocking reality that without Him she could do nothing. At this point, she left her water pot and ran into the city to witness to those who once had rejected and shunned her that a "real man" --Jesus had changed her life.

So we, too, must lay aside every weight, and we, too, must forget those things behind us and press toward the prize of the high calling of God in Christ Jesus. We, too, now God's women, must leave our water pots. Our water pots of insecurity, inferiority, inadequacy, anger, depression, unforgiveness, bitterness, underlying hostility, and all of our past pains and misery. We must now hear what the Spirit has to say and depart from the lies of Satan. We must depart from our former ways and lifestyles to measure up to the standards of the Most High God.

When we find ourselves interested in a natural

man, we sometimes take extreme measures to impress him. We clean our homes thoroughly, take extra pains with our appearance, buy new clothes, or whatever else it takes to endear him to us. Likewise, we must now strive to be found pleasing in God's sight.

Our self-image is also based on our hopes and ambitions. We know what we want to be and that we can be given the wealth of resources we have within us. The Lord spoke to my heart and instructed me to tell his daughters that each of them possess a gift that can sustain them financially. I am saying that your wealth lies within you. If you tapped into it, you could support yourselves and your family and enjoy doing it. I'm not talking about working for someone else. Some of you at this reading are unemployed, and the enemy is trying to convince you that you are a failure and will be destroyed. He's a liar. You have marketable talents and skills. If you seek God, you will find what you have within you to sustain you and to finance your vision.

The third image we walk in is the image God has of us. The image He had in His mind when He created us. Knowing that He has chosen to create us like unto Himself, we realize that He expects us to reflect to the world His character and His righteousness. Because we are like Him, we have several attributes He expects us to show forth.

As Jesus told the Samaritan woman, "God is Spirit." Because we have been changed from death unto life, we must now seek the things of the Spirit rather than the things of the flesh.

"If ye then be risen with Christ, seek those things which are above, where Christ sitteth on the right hand of God. Set your affection on things above, not on things on the earth. For ye are dead, and your life is hid with Christ in God. When Christ, who is our life, shall appear, then shall ye also appear with him in glory" (Colossians 3:1-4).

Although God's Word tells us that we are created in God's spirit image and we are to reckon our flesh to be dead, in many instances we continue to sow to the flesh. The Lord led me to know that many women are afflicted and in bondage on jobs outside of their homes because of their fleshly desires. He told me that if some of us would submit to our husbands, we would not have to work to be sustained. But because of our lust for things—nice clothing, elaborate homes, late-model cars, and a desire to pamper ourselves at spas and beauty salons—we spend most of our time working when we could be at home resting in Him. Often our husbands can support us; we must, however, be willing to live within their means.

God says to us today that His way is still the best way. Paul instructs us to conform no longer to this world system but to be transformed. Time and time again, I hear women say how they would do anything to stay home, nurture the children, and run the house. It is God's Will for women to be homemakers. It is a biblical principle. However, we must come to grips with the fact that this entails sacrifice. It means giving up the standards of the world and coming up to the standards of God.

The spirit man must reign in our lives. The only way that this is going to take place is that we strengthen him by feeding him God's Word. We concern ourselves with rendering due benevolence to our husbands in the natural, but God spoke to my heart saying that we as His women do not give Him His benevolence. We neglect Him when we do not commune with Him in prayer and neglect His Word or when we are slack on our meditation and fellowship with Him. He says that in our attempt to serve Him by being busy about His business, we have left Him behind. The problem today is that we try to fit Him into our lives rather than placing our lives in Him, for He cannot be contained.

Another attribute that should show forth in our lives is holiness. "Be ye holy, for I am holy." Without holiness we shall not see the Lord. We shall not behold His face after all of our church going, tithe paying, Sunday School teaching, choir singing and ushering—even our chicken frying unless we live holy lives. We must walk apart from this world in righteousness. Being good is not being holy. Holiness comes forth only from the Holy Ghost as it sanctifies us daily.

The first chapter of Genesis says, "And God said let us make man." God has revealed His character and His essence to Israel through His Name. The names of God give us the understanding of who He is and what He can do and will do. Here God is Elohim the Creator God. We as God's women now have creative ability.

So many aspects of God's creative being leave me in awe. The movement of God's Spirit on the composers like Mozart, Liszt, Rachmaninoff, and others who have translated God's thoughts into musical notes, thereby allowing mortals to experience God as Composer, I am speechless. When I, like David, look at the heavens and ponder the intricacy with which He designs snowflakes, no two ever being alike, yet all having six points of equal length and each consisting of a conglomeration of ice crystals, I am breathless. As an interior decorator, I bow to Him and honor Him as the Master Decorator knowing that my designs are expressions of His creativity. But as the mother of seven, I experience the creativity of Elohim most vividly in my children. I am amazed that God can take two people and use their genetic design to produce an infinite number of offspring, each unique in personality, emotion, psychology, and physiology.

"And God blessed them, and God said unto them, Be fruitful, and multiply, and replenish the earth, and subdue it: and have dominion over the fish of the sea, and over the fowl of the air, and over every living thing that moveth upon the earth" (Genesis 1:28).

I know this may sound strange coming from the mother of seven children, but being fruitful is not about having a bunch of babies. It is about being creative, productive, and resourceful. When we allow God to develop our creative potential to its fullest, we move beyond being biological mothers and become the nurturers and life-givers that He intended for us to be. Our creative expression and our power of influence seasoned by the Holy Spirit enables us to subdue the earth and have dominion over every living creature.

Finally, God is sovereign. As God's women, we are rulers. God commanded Moses to conquer the land by dispossessing the enemy. He told Joshua, "Every place that the sole of your foot shall tread upon, that have I given unto you, as I said unto Moses. . . . There shall not any man be able to stand before thee all the days of thy life: as I was with Moses, so I will be with thee. . . ." Our land is our home, our job space, the bus stop--wherever we stand, we are in possession, we are in authority.

So often in ministering to God's women, it becomes apparent that they are not walking and ruling with the power of God. They have not taken hold of the authority God has given them. This is obvious in the homes of many in which the teenagers are in control. We should take authority over our children when they leave the womb, not when they begin to embarrass us. It is our responsibility and duty to God as the keepers of the home to rear our children to become responsible and independent.

We must examine the emotional needs of the woman who insists that her children remain dependent and in the nest pass adulthood. We all are acquainted with families of adults in which only the parents contribute to the household and support the needs, wants, and habits of their king-sized kids. Verily, verily I say unto you, one day you will have to leave this earth. How do you suppose your thirty-five-year-old son or daughter will fare if you have never confronted him or her with the reality of your mortality nor committed unto them the responsibility of providing for themselves.

Likewise, we need to take authority in the workplace. God's women should not be allowing the enemy to abuse and sexually harass them. It is not God's will for His daughters to be in the workplace; however, if we are there, we should be the influencing factor among the unsaved. As the woman determines the climate of the home, so should she influence the work environment. God has declared that no man will be able to come against us when we stand for Him. When God's women begin to cry out and say no more harassment, no more abuse, and no more sexism, there will be no more. God is on our side. He will stand with us and go before us to pave the way. We must, like Israel, under the counsel of God, believe Him to give us the victory.

CHAPTER FOUR

PREPARING FOR A CHRISTIAN MARRIAGE

As we determined in the previous chapter, we must separate ourselves from those who consider themselves Christian because their family is Christian, they live in a Christian nation, or the church they attend is Christian. Our topic refers to those who obey Christian doctrine. Therefore, when we refer to a Christian marriage we speak of the union between two born-again, spirit-filled people living a holy life. We are not speaking of those acquainted with the Lord through scripture because they attended Sunday School as children or people who are merely good citizens. We are speaking of those led by the Spirit of God.

Subsequently, the first step in preparing for a Christian marriage is to give your life to Christ. Many women actually come to God's house in search of "Mr. Right." They substitute the church for singles' bars. Before we can see what God sees for us, we must have the mind of Christ. We overlook the blessings God has for us whenever we are not spirit-led; for the things of the Spirit do not appeal to the flesh. The man you would select for yourself based on your fleshly responses is not the man God would choose for you.

The next step is to prepare for a change in lifestyle and in relationships. I talk to many young women who lived the "good life" before marriage or were used to pampering themselves. Once they married and financial responsibility became an inescapable reality, they no longer felt excited about holy matrimony. Younger women, in particular, find it difficult to accept that their wardrobes can no longer be priority and the rent must be paid at the risk of sacrificing the upkeep of hair and nails.

"Therefore shall a man leave his father and his mother, and shall cleave unto his wife: and they shall be one flesh" (Genesis 2:24).

God has made it clear that our husbands are our first priority. Our relationship with our friends and families must change. Many times, women put their children's wants before their husbands' needs. God's Word says, not so. Children are by-products of marriage, and this must be kept in perspective for the relationship between husband and wife to thrive.

We must now lay aside the demands and dictates of our best friends, mothers, associates, and others whom we cherish and turn our hearts and minds toward developing a deep and lasting relationship with our husbands. We should not engage in lengthy telephone conversations and frequent visits with our friends when our husbands are waiting for our attention. Often the lines of communication between husband and wife breakdown because wives invest more time in their friends then they do in their spouses.

When we were single, some of us developed friendships with and loyalties to men other than our husbands. We now must adjust to the inevitable change in those friendships. Most men have problems accepting that their wives' best friends are other men. Continuing the friendship can only give Satan a toe hold to destroy your new marriage. Consequently, you may have to say to your men friends, "We are friends. I love you dearly. You have contributed a lot to my life, but I am getting married. Stay away!" The typical man will not appreciate another man holding a place of intimacy in his wife's life. Although he may say it's okay, it's not. He may say he understands, but he doesn't. Use wisdom. Get rid of the acquaintances. Otherwise, your husband will manifest his dismay by acting out at some other place in the marriage.

Prepare to wait for your mate. Often, we want God to do a fast thing in our lives about marriage. So often I hear women say, "I know the Lord sent this man to me because he is exactly what I prayed for." Satan knows our prayers. He hears our conversations with others. Satan, more than likely, will conjure a counterfeit and present it to you before God sends you His blessing. Satan's deception is the reason it is a necessity for us to allow God to develop the prayer language--the ability to pray in the Spirit--in our lives, so we can exclude Satan from our communion with God.

Those of us who feel unfulfilled unless we have a man are "easy pickin's" for the enemy. He knows that keeping a man before us will be a sufficient deterrent to our growth and walk with God. These women move from one failed romantic relationship to the next, proclaiming that the "Lawd" says this is my husband.

Along these same lines, some of us develop relationships too easily with men based on our assumption of their salvation. We believe every demon who says, "I love the Lord." The Bible says that the Queen of Sheba heard of Solomon's awesomeness and went to see for herself. We must follow her example. For not only did she go to see and investigate what she had heard about him, she also questioned him. She asked Solomon everything that was in her heart, and he satisfied her inquiries. Some of us accept anything presented to us and take too many things for granted or at face value. It ain't necessarily so!

Frequently, we allow ourselves to be fooled--deceived by "church going" brothers. You need to look these guys in their eyes and not ask them whether they are saved, but whether they are filled with the Holy Ghost. Anyone who cannot readily tell you yes should not be on your dating list. Anyone unchurched should not be on your dating list. Anyone who does not put God first should not be on your dating list. Now you may ask, what's the big deal? As long as he's a good person what difference does it make whether he's a fanatic for Jesus? Marriage is sacred. It depicts the relationship between Christ and the Church. It is the ultimate relationship. It is the highest form of intimacy. God is so serious about the marriage that His word indicates that we (the Church) will be presented to Christ as His bride.

"Be ye not unequally yoked together with unbelievers: for what fellowship hath righteousness with unrighteousness? and what communion hath light with darkness? And what concord hath Christ with Belial? or what part hath he that believeth with an infidel?" (II Corinthians 6:14-15)

It is important for us to accept the cold, hard fact that the unbeliever is the son of Satan. If we realize that, our perspective on the matter of marrying an unbeliever must change. Remember, we wrestle not with flesh and blood. It is not about how nice a man is, his prestigious position in life, or his promises to you; it is about principalities, powers, and spiritual weakness in high places.

When God says no to a marriage and we run off to the Justice of the Peace and marry anyway, we have merely secured a license from man to sin against God. For the Word of God declares that no man can bless what He curses. If your marriage is not sanctioned by God and sealed by the Holy Spirit, it doesn't matter who attended the wedding or in what fine church it was held. Disobeying God does not change His mind or His stand on the issue.

Some women feel that everything is okay if they marry an unsaved man and the marriage seems to be working out, according to man's standards. God does not look at our rebellion and say, "Oh well, they're doing fine, so everything is okay with Me." He looks at us with grief in His heart, for He must honor His Word, which means He cannot extend the fullest benefits of His blessings because of our disobedience.

The enemy of our souls has deceived us into believing that once the wedding is over God forgives us, and it is business as usual. Marriage is not an act but a condition or state of existence. Therefore, we are now walking in a diminished state before God. Our standing cannot be changed in that it was secured by the redeeming love of God and we were purchased by the Blood of Jesus. However, we determine our state, and our state fluctuates according to our circumstances and situations. Consequently, we have violated our covenant with God and come under the authority of Satan--for the unbeliever is our authority and his authority is Satan. For if Christ is the head of man and man is the head of woman, then Satan is the head of the unbeliever. And the demonically influenced unbeliever is the head of his wife. For the kingdom of God is based on principles, unaltered to accommodate our disobedience. God's principles say that man is the head of woman, and woman is subject to her husband. In short, in marrying an unbeliever, you are throwing away your inheritance.

I have been challenged with the premise that God can change anyone, and who says He won't save my boyfriend after we marry. Who says He will save your boyfriend after you marry? Some people are not predestined to receive salvation. Heaven help you if you have picked one of them.

We must also be mindful that a saved man does not ensure a perfect union. We accept the principle of being unequally yoked spiritually. However, there is also the reality of our being unequally yoked financially, educationally, socially, etc. You must consider all aspects of the marriage once it has been established that a brother is truly a believer. You must consider all facts. You must examine all matters.

Even though you both may love the Lord, there may be some variables in the marriage you may not be able to resolve. Sometimes family backgrounds and lifestyles are unable to blend. It is most difficult for educated, well-paid women to accept undereducated, underemployed men. The first thing that comes up in a heated discussion is this issue, which, of course, can be quite devastating to either party. So if you're a Harvard graduate with a doctorate in Law, I don't think a jackleg plumber would be a wise choice.

We must learn to allow God time to show us about these brothers. You have time. If he's yours, you don't have to worry about rushing into marriage. You need to observe your prospective husbands and take notice of their behavior before you extend yourselves to them. Watch and pray. Is he faithful? Does he follow his vision? Does he have a vision? How does he treat others? How does he handle conflict and confrontation? What is he like with other women? Is he loose? How does he express his anger and disappointment? Is he modest or is he flashy?

These are serious questions. You are selecting a partner for life. When you come before God in matrimony you are asking Him to receive you and your groom as one. Therefore, you want to eliminate the possibility of ending up with the "worst, the poorest, and the sickest." If you are obedient to God's criteria for a marriage partner, you save yourselves heartache and a trip to divorce court.

Usually about this time I hear the question, "What am I to do about my sexual urges while I'm waiting for this picture perfect man of God? I am a healthy mature woman. How do I handle my desires?" The Word of God tells us that a single woman can attend to the matters of God without distraction (I Corinthians 7). So first of all, I suggest that you get up, turn off the television, put down your potato chips and get busy. Be about the Father's business. Leave no time and no energy for Satan to get in your ear and tell you that your flesh needs gratification.

Stay away from jeopardizing situations when you anticipate being alone with a man, for I am sure you know your limits. Turn your ear away from love music. It feeds the flesh. God says He wants us to make melody in our hearts unto Him with hymns, psalms, and spiritual songs. Love ballads sing of adoration of man rather than God. We all know He's a Jealous God.

Next, you must learn to take control of your thought life. We allow Satan to seduce us in our minds. Some of the love music that we listen to literally sings our panties right off. If you're wondering why your sexual urges are so pronounced, it may be because you're playing "love" music all night and programming yourselves to respond sexually.

I often tease single sisters when we're in exclusively women's settings by suggesting they begin to wear "holely" undergarments on their dates rather then silk teddies and over-priced lingerie, for one is more reluctant to undress for a man under those circumstances. I know when I spend fifty dollars on an undergarment, someone is going to see it. Fortunately for me there is a Reverend Mr. Jennings. Just a tidbit.

Also, avoid long-term engagements. I suggest this because long engagements may result in fornication. After observing your prospective husband and determining he is eligible by the Word of God, be prepared to marry quickly. For if the Holy Spirit has confirmed that this marriage is ordained by God, don't prolong the engagement. And please know that God will confirm His will for the marriage in both of you. Don't trust some nut who walks up to you and says, "God said you are my wife." You should know as well.

Casual dating is the way of the world. If you are not expecting God to bless you with a husband, there is no reason for you to be just hanging out with men for lack of something better to do. Shun the appearance of evil. Although you may say, "I'm not doing anything wrong," to your brothers and sisters in Christ, it looks as if you are "flip-flopping," as my mommy would say.

Finally, sexual fulfillment is no reason to seek marriage. Sexual gratification should be the result of a healthy marriage, not the reason for the marriage. There are married women who are not satisfied sexually and that can be a bigger problem than being single. I am sure experienced, single women will agree that the only thing worse then being hot and bothered is to be hot and having to be bothered with someone who just fuels the fire but can't quench it.

Prepare to submit. Submit meaning to yield or surrender, placing things in their proper order. The fifth chapter of Ephesians tells us to submit to our husbands as unto the Lord. Whenever I speak the "S" word, I feel a not so subtle resistance. I attribute this to our not having been taught the significance of this command. Although some use God's Word as a tool to oppress and humiliate women, we must know that God in His infinite wisdom and knowledge has arranged for His daughters to be kept like queens if we obey His word.

We should not be offended by the word submit. Jesus made it clear that he had submitted himself to the Will of the Father. However, Paul tells us that He counted it not robbery to be equal with God. Submission does not make us a lesser. We can submit and maintain our integrity and equality as humans. God commanded men and women to be fruitful, multiply, replenish the earth, and subdue it (Genesis 1:28); however, there is an organizational chart in Glory.

Order is the first rule of God's Kingdom. His order designates specific tasks to men and women. We have our functions, duties, and responsibilities. To the men, He designated provision and protection. Protection is not always a show of brute force, but a covering. Sometimes when I am in the field and my husband is not with me, a lustful preacher will ask whether I'm married. When I say yes, he backs off. My husband, though absent, has just protected me. He has shielded me from the adversary. To women, God left instruction through Paul that we bear children and guide the house. God's preference is that the woman work at home.

When all things are in line with God's Word with regard to our romantic and marriage lives, we find submission a gift and a blessing from God. I say that all things must be in line with God's Word, for if we, as His daughters, disobey and allow ourselves to enter into covenant with a man against God's choosing, we will suffer dearly. It is a natural response for a woman to submit to one in whom she can place her trust. I would dare to say that there is not a woman alive who would not willingly and completely surrender to one whom she knows hearkens to the voice of God and one who she knows will do, at all costs, what is best for her and her family.

For many of us, disobedience has left us in financial ruin, emotional devastation, and spiritual bankruptcy. For this reason I say most emphatically to my single sisters, marry a Holy Ghost-filled man of God. If the man you are involved with is not saved, get over it! Your fleshly lusts will not endure the hell for which you are setting yourselves up for.

Marrying an unsaved man places you in the hands of an intercessor who has no favor in the eyes of God. Whereas you were able to boldly approach the throne of grace in your singlehood, now you have a priest who stands not in the authority of God. Because your head has no favor with God, you are left to depend on God's mercy and rendered inaccessible to His Perfect Will for your life. Because God is a God of order, he distributes the family's blessings through the man. If your husband is not a man of God, you have blocked your flow of abundance. Therefore, not only may you be found having to support yourself and a man in the natural but also you will find that you are sharing your spiritual resources because the unsaved has not an inheritance of his own.

In other words, whereas you should be partaking of the benefits of two inheritances, you will now have to split or share your inheritance with the unbeliever, thereby living beneath your privilege. And believe it or not, if you choose to go against God and marry an unsaved man, you must still submit. And you know what else? Divorce is not an option. For although God has not blessed the marriage nor does He reign in it, you still entered into covenant. For better or worse, remember?

We must now prepare for Satanic attack. More often than not, our marriages become the devil's playgrounds. The more complex our lives become, the more areas he has to work in. The marriage is good ground for him to sow the seeds of affliction and tribulation. Satan is going to attack you through the marriage. You can count on that. It is his plan to get you to doubt your decision to wed and thereby attempt to tear down the marriage.

All right, now that you have prepared yourselves, I will share with you the qualifications that you should look for in a man that will increase the probability of a successful marriage. When I speak of of success in marriage, I speak qualitatively and not quantitatively. In other words a fifty-year marriage is not necessarily indicative of a successful one. We don't want to become like an old shoe to our spouses and find ourselves stuck in a dead and empty marriage in our later years. But we want vitality and happiness to abide even after the children are grown and married.

So remember, HE DOESN'T QUALIFY IF . . .

1. He's not a spirit-filled believer.
2. He's married (this includes being separated).
3. He can not support you financially.
4. He doesn't like the way you look, act, or dress.
5. He thinks his needs are more important than yours.
6. He loves another woman.
7. He doesn't want to get married.
8. You don't really like him, but you're desperate and he has a good job or good connections.
9. You don't really like him, but your family does.
10. You want children, and he doesn't or vice versa.
11. You're only interested in him for his looks, material possessions, or the body chemistry you feel between you.
12. The Lord has not told you he's the one.

Although looks and passion are helpful, we want to avoid finding ourselves wedded to a good-looking, sweet-smelling devil. Good sex is wonderful but it still doesn't buy groceries and most young marriages fail because of financial hardship. Be wise, think long term. Be blessed!

CHAPTER FIVE

THE LIES MEN TELL

There is a scenario in Second Samuel, the thirteenth chapter that I find tragic yet relevant to all young women. I am concerned about the web of deception into which our teenaged daughters and sisters are falling, leaving them damaged and devastated to enter womanhood as broken and marred vessels.

Although we know that God can pick up the pieces of our lives and restore us before His presence, sometimes the consequences of our mistakes leave us without the benefits and blessings which God has decreed for us.

It is with this in mind that I dedicate this chapter to my young sisters all over the world.

King David had a son named Amnon and a daughter named Tamar. Amnon and Tamar had different mothers. Amnon loved Tamar but knew he could not have her sexually because she was a virgin. He became so obsessed with having her that he worked himself into a frenzy and made himself sick.

Sometimes we can think we want something so badly that we feel we'll die if we don't have it. Satan wants to trick us and get us to the point that we will lie, steal, cheat, or kill to have what we want. But remember, nothing or no one will last forever. So count the cost. Is it worth all that?

Amnon had a friend who advised him how to get Tamar. He suggested that Amnon pretend that he was sick and ask King David to send Tamar to take care of him. David trusted Amnon because Amnon was his son and Tamar's brother. So David agreed and commanded Tamar to go to Amnon's room. Although most parents can detect whether a young man has good intentions, sometimes young men can be very deceptive.

Once Tamar got to Amnon's room he put everyone out and raped her. Before Amnon raped her, Tamar begged him to do the right thing and ask the king for permission to marry her, but he would not. After he raped her, the Bible says he hated her and commanded that she be taken away and the door locked behind her. He didn't want her. He didn't want to see her or to hear her cry of despair. Tamar tore off her virgin clothes and held her head in shame.

Your virginity is of great value. It is God's

desire that young men and women remain sexually pure or virgins until they marry. How old you are does not determine whether or not you should be sexually active. Marriage makes that determination. Your husband will love and appreciate you much more when he knows that you have given yourself only to him in that special way.

There are times when we let our guard down because of a person's upbringing or family background, but we must be watchful for subtle behavior that signals to us that there is a problem.

Some warning signs you should not ignore are (a) young men who like to play by slapping you or punching you (once they feel you belong to them the slaps and punches become real); (b) the young man who never has money (they will always take and never give; they usually become husbands who refuse to work and pay bills); (c) The men who always seem more interested in your sisters and girlfriends than they are in you (they usually become adulterers and are unfaithful throughout marriage); and finally, (d) the men who disrespect their mother and sisters (these men dislike women and are users). Stay away. The way a man looks, and the car he drives should not determine whether he's dating material; his character should be the measuring stick.

You should be uncomfortable with a man who always wants to be alone with you. His always wanting to be alone with you is a sure sign that he wants to pressure you into having sex. Men are stronger than women. Telling them no is not enough. They can physically overpower you and take your body. You should know that kissing and caressing a boy's body prepares him for sex. If you expect to remain a virgin or desire to live holy and sexually pure before God, you must understand that necking and petting is forbidden. Otherwise, your body will crave sex, and it will be just a matter of time before you will give in to those yearnings.

The problem with our teens today is that they have no shame. Not too long ago, for young women to have children out of wedlock was a disgrace. For a young woman to be seen in public kissing, cuddling, or showing the faintest hint of intimacy dishonored the family. My mother became extremely upset one day because a boy put his arm around my shoulder as we walked home from school.

Now it is not unusual to see young teens embracing and kissing at the bus stops or leaning on cars with their bodies interlocked like snakes during mating season.

Satan has perpetuated a fraud that being sexually active is cool and a sign of maturity. Sexual activity among unmarried teens is irresponsible and stupid. God created sex to be enjoyed by married couples for the purpose of having children. In modern day society, men will say and do anything to get you to go to bed with them. And once you do, sooner or later they will drop you. Here is a list of lies men tell to rob you of your virginity, your sense of self-worth, and your integrity. Remember, pretty clothes and fancy hairdos cannot replace your honor. Getting pregnant is not a smart way to get even with your parents. You only hurt yourself.

The Lies Men Tell

1. I love you.
2. You're the most beautiful creature I've ever seen.
3. You're so intelligent. I want to make love to your mind.
4. If you love me, you will prove it.
5. Let's just do it one time.
6. I'll stop when you tell me to.
7. You can't get pregnant the first time.
8. I've never felt this way about anyone else.
9. I'll marry you if you do it.
10. I won't tell anyone.
11. It's okay because we love each other.
12. Age is just a number. If we care for each other it doesn't matter how old I am.
13. You're just scared. Maybe you're not as mature as I thought.
14. God is love, and we're making love so he doesn't mind.
15. Marriages are made in heaven, so we're already married.
16. You must be gay.

The Lies Married Men Tell

1. I'm not married. She's my roommate.
2. I love her, but I'm not in love with her.
3. I need you to help me stay with her.
4. You fill the void in my life.
5. My wife and I have an understanding. She goes her way and I go mine.
6. We're just together for the kids.
7. Our marriage died years ago.
8. We're getting a divorce.
9. We have property together, and we have to work things out.
10. If I leave her, she won't be able to handle it.
11. She's been good to me, so I have to help her get on her feet before I leave her.
12. I don't have a telephone at home, so you have to call me at work.
13. She doesn't satisfy me.
14. My wife has another man.
15. She says she doesn't love me and wants me out of her life
16. My wife is selfish and doesn't care about anything but getting what she wants.
17. This is the first time I have ever had an affair.
18. I'm going to tell her about us soon.
19. I wasn't saved when we married, so she's not really my wife.

CHAPTER SIX

MINISTERING TO YOUR HUSBAND

"Wives, submit yourselves unto your own husbands, as unto the Lord"(Ephesians 5:22).

"As unto the Lord!" I have found it most effective to present to the sisterhood the hypothetical situation of our beings married to Jesus in the flesh. This immediately bring into focus the reality that we have yet to become the wives that God would have us be. Even those of us who boast of being modern day June Cleavers and Betty Crockers must take a second look at our domestic prowess when we stand in the light of this reality.

When we view our marriages as if we were married to Christ, it becomes obvious to us that we have fallen short of God's glory. Many of us have jewels for husbands, but we have not yielded the authority to them that God says they should have. For example, some of our husbands are not meeting their financial responsibilities because they know we will jump the gun and do it ourselves. We have created our own monster.

Many of us are frustrated and overworked because we attempt to fill our shoes and our husbands'. We want what we want, when we want it. So we usurp authority and treat our husband as if they were children. If they don't respond the way we want them to, we "do it ourselves." Subsequently, we place ourselves in bondage and create a barrier between ourselves and our husbands.

Sometimes we make our mistakes at the beginning of our marriages. We start out wrong. Some of us are so happy to get a husband that we go too far when it comes to determining the division of labor. We should never volunteer to pay the rent or mortgage. Now, mind you, if you marry a man who earns less than $20,000 per year you should be prepared to live within his income. Otherwise, it is not fair for you to expect him to provide you with a $75,000 lifestyle, or for you to complain about sharing in the housing expenses. We must be reasonable.

In all fairness, I must say that being saved will not necessarily determine that a man will be a good husband, nor does being unsaved render a man poor husband material in all cases. For I know women married to unsaved men who rule their homes well. I also know of too many believers who are financially irresponsible, poor providers, and negligent and abusive husbands. Sad to say, financial irresponsibility is also true among many pastors and other church leaders as well. I cringe when I hear increasing numbers of starry-eyed wives of bishops, pastors, and deacons say, "It's alright for my husband to neglect the family and not support us financially because he's such a man of God and he's giving all of his money and time and attention to the church." Now tell me, what is wrong with that picture!

Not only must we learn to stay in the line of authority about the financial matters of the home, but also we must now learn to stay in the line of authority in the matters of God. Too often we jump between God and our husbands to negate God's dealing with them the way He must to get our husbands to be the men they need to be. MOVE! If we let God have His Way with our husbands, even though that may mean our suffering for a season, as well, our lives will be made richer. Unfortunately, it may take a supernatural pistol whipping to get your husband to fall in line with God's Word.

Again, we realize that we must trust God before we can submit to man. We must trust Him to the extent that we know that regardless of what's taking place between Him and our husbands He will see to it that we and our children are provided for. Submission is an act of faith. We serve God through submission to our husbands. I know for some of us this is truly a faith walk. This is not something that takes place overnight. Know that it may mean re-learning behavior, behavior we learned from the strong women of our ancestry who taught us to trust no one and to look out for our own interests. Submission is a process, a spiritual process. For as Christ increases in us and we grow in maturity and are strengthened in our walk with Him, we can then trust him in the lives of our men.

In the course of my presenting this teaching at a women's retreat, a woman raised her hand at this point and asked, "What if your husband is not saved?" You must still treat him as if he were.

"Likewise, ye wives, be in subjection to your own husbands; that, if any obey not the word, they also may without the word be won by the conversation of the wives; while they behold your chaste conversation coupled with fear" (I Peter 3: 1-2).

Our homes are our vineyards. I know many powerhouses for the Lord who stand as intercessors and exercise deliverance ministries in the household of faith. Yet in their own their homes, they have no endurance. This ought not to be so.

"But ye shall receive power, after that the Holy Ghost is come upon you: and ye shall be witnesses unto me both in Jerusalem, and in all Judea, and in Samaria, and unto the uttermost part of the earth" (Acts 1:8).

Jerusalem is the home place. There are too many sisters today claiming to love the Lord who are not willing to stand in the gap for their unsaved husbands. They say such things as, "I want him saved, but I don't want him as a husband." Do you really care if he's saved? If you do you will labor in prayer and intercession for him. If you want him saved, you will do battle with Satan and he will be your priority rather than those whom you don't know.

Satan has told too many of us that our husbands' being unsaved exonerates us from the responsibility of our marriages and justifies our having another man. Satan is a liar! That's his job. That is all he does is lie! Lie! Lie!

Some of us are satisfied with our husbands' being unsaved because their salvation would bring a new dimension to the marriage. For once our husbands know the truth and study God's Word, they may soon realize that we are not living up to our responsibilities to them as wives. God will hold us accountable for our soul winning efforts or lack of them regarding our husbands.

Many of us are in denial. We refuse to accept that God can perform miracles in our marriages and make them testimonies that He is a Deliverer. We are in denial because we are not willing to pay the price. We are not willing to suffer. We are not willing to lay down our lives. We say we are sold out to God, but have we truly turned our marriages over to him? Are we cooperating with God for the salvation of our unsaved husbands?

Back to submission. We know that some of us are not in ideal situations. Some of us are married to substance abusers, gamblers, and others who cannot be trusted to handle the family finances. Be realistic. I have met women who did not want to accept that they did not have financial problems—they had husband problems. Wake Up! Smell the coffee! If your husband is a thief, don't leave your credit cards, bank card, jewelry, and mortgage money lying around. If your husband is a drug addict, until he is delivered, stop trusting him to make your bank deposits!

Face reality and make the necessary adjustments in your life. If you love your husband and you want to stay with him, that's okay. It's biblical. "For better or for worse." Sometimes we get the worse. Just be realistic. In due season, God will prevail. Stop listening to frustrated old ladies and busybody friends who say, "If it was my husband, I'd leave him." No they wouldn't. That's why they're stuck in a rut in their marriages.

On the other hand, we must seek the Lord and use wisdom when we find ourselves in danger or the safety and well-being of our children jeopardized. Likewise, some people will sit on the sidelines, call the plays for your marriage, and tell you that even though you're battered and your children are abused that you should stay. Seek the Lord's counsel.

"I will therefore that the younger women marry, bear children, guide the house, give none occasion to the adversary to speak reproachfully" (I Timothy 5:14).

Guess what! This scripture does not enslave you. Guiding the house means you are a home manager. Being a home manager means that it is your responsibility to see that things are done, but not necessarily that you have to do them. We may not all be able to afford professional housekeepers; however, some of us have children who can assist us whom we have not trained to do so. If you teach your children at an early age to carry their load, life would be much easier for you as they get older. Designate. The ability to designate tasks separates the great leaders from the overworked ones. Any household with teenagers should be clean if you do your job in rearing them to become responsible and independent. I know it's difficult. I know they can get rebellious, so can you. No wash dishes, no movie money. Let them know that completing their household chores is their first introduction to the job world. You owe them that.

Some of us are blessed with husbands who enjoy sharing domestic responsibilities. Take advantage of the blessing. No law says the husbands can't help. Even in housekeeping, there is a division of labor. God is holding you responsible for managing the family system, not for doing it all yourselves. If your husband can cook and enjoys it, that's fine. What you agree to in your marriage is between the two of you and God. I have no right to say what should or should not take place in your home if the two of you are in agreement and it works for your family. I know that we have been taught that because we are the women, sick or well, we cook, clean, wash, iron, sew, teach, take care of the children, and tend to the needs and wants of our husbands. If, and only if, there is time left, we can do something for ourselves. If we do not take time for ourselves, we won't be any good to anyone else. I'm not speaking of days away from home, not even hours. However, we need to take mental health breaks.

I know what it is like to get caught up in the family system and to lose yourself. By the time my seventh child was born, an uninterrupted shower was equivalent to a trip to the Bahamas. Everyone in my household knows, if you want to see the beast in Mommy just knock on the bathroom door when she's in the shower. Cheese and Crackers! That drives me bananas. Why. Because it's my time, my time of reflection, my time of quiet, my time to pamper myself and regroup for the next shift. Take your time. Demand your time. Write it into the family schedule. Work it into the baby-sitter's hours. Do whatever it takes to get it, and don't compromise unless it is absolutely necessary. When you compromise your time, others no longer take your time seriously and you will lose it.

Enough about us, now let's focus on our topic of "ministering to our husbands." As women, we know quite well what it feels like to have unmet needs and to have areas of our lives lie untouched year after year. We know what it means to want those needs touched or ministered to by the ones closest to us, our husbands. Well guess what, they feel the same way about us. Much to our chagrin, we cannot be all things to our husbands; however, we must attempt to satisfy them more than we do.

Everyday I talk to married women starving for romance, women who want passion and courtship. Subsequently, Satan has trapped some of our sisters in adultery as a result of their search for passion. I declare unto you, God can restore the passion in your marriage if you learn to minister to your husband effectively.

TIPS FOR MINISTERING TO YOUR HUSBAND

Forgive Him. The first step in ministering to your husband is to forgive him. Nothing you can do will be successful in restoring your marriage if you don't strengthen the foundation. A marriage built on the broken foundation of unforgiveness is superficial and sure to collapse before long. Many of us must first work on the hidden scars and unhealed wounds covered by smiles and an accumulation of "things" before we get new hairdo's, fancy lingerie, or expensive perfumes in an attempt to woo our men. We cannot speak "forgive" without its companion "forget." We, as God did for us, must "choose not to remember" the sins of our husbands against us that we may be delivered and our marriages healed.

Understand Him. Next, we must reclaim our husbands and their affections. We can be successful in ministering to our husbands if we realize they are

different from us. They don't think like we do.
They don't feel the way we feel. Men can become
consumed by or preoccupied with external issues
that lure them away from their emotional concerns
whereas our emotional concerns override our other
issues.

Pray For Him. Based on this fact we must
redirect the traffic of their thinking and detour them
with our affection. We have different adversaries
when it comes to this area. Some of us compete with
other women, jobs, sports, ministries, automobiles,
mothers-in-law, step-children, buddies, and the list
goes on and on. Here is where our prayer lives are
instrumental. We must petition God to give us favor
in the eyes of our husbands. We must intercede and
come against the strongholds the enemy has placed
in our marriages and know that God wills it to be so
and can perform it.

Woo Him. In the reclaiming process we must
not only use our prayer power but sharpen and exercise our lovemaking skills more frequently. Believe
it or not, prayer power and lovemaking can work
hand in hand. The Word of God presents to us the
effectiveness of anointing and laying on of hands.
Anointing and laying on of hands can be accom-
plished in our marriages during our lovemaking.
Notice I said lovemaking. Lovemaking is the key to
success. Make love to your husband and stop just
having sex. Lovemaking is the God given avenue
for us to minister to our husbands' bodies. God's

Word commands us to give due benevolence. And I might add that we should give cheerfully, not begrudgingly. Our lovemaking should not be a sacrifice but a freewill offering. Satan has particularly deceived us about lovemaking by having us believe that by refusing to meet our husbands' sexual needs, we have control of the situation. What he has succeeded in doing is breaking our fellowship with our husbands and leading us into transgression against God.

Anoint Him. As we minister to our husbands' bodies, we can simultaneously anoint him and pray for his deliverance. Here's how. Prepare him a temperature-perfect bath. Either share it with him, which is the best time for conversation, or if you choose not to get in, bathe him yourself. It is very important that you bathe him with your hands. Do not use a washcloth. He will not resist. Use the tender care you would use with your newborn child. If you decide to get in with him, you might want to bring his favorite snack or dessert along and feed it to him. After you bathe him, pat him dry. Patting is important because it relaxes further and pampers the body. Buy a jumbo-size towel or bath blanket to use only for this occasion.

Use a heated skin softening agent like your favorite lotion or baby oil and, beginning with each individual toe, massage his body from bottom to top. Take your time. As you massage him, pray over every area and reclaim it to the Lord and to your

in that capacity.

There may be times when we feel that we have clearer visions than our husbands. I have learned that when we trust God in our husbands and yield to their visions, God honors their faith and will perfect the vision as it unfolds and the fullness thereof is far greater than our expectations. Remember, He can do exceeding abundantly above all that we ask or think.

When we grasp our husbands' visions, it will make plain the vision and purpose that God has for our lives, for when we are yoked, by God, with a man, the yoke is for the purpose of the gospel. Therefore, we are fitly joined and two become one, complimenting and enhancing one another.

God's vision for your husband includes you. Sometimes it is necessary for us to "harness" our husbands' visions. For many of us have desires that God has placed in our hearts that we just consider silly ideas. In listening to our husbands, we will soon discover that certain subjects may be addressed frequently but quickly dismissed. Quite possibly, these are viable visions.

Reassure and Comfort Him. We must also learn to minister to our husbands' emotional needs. Encouraging them, standing beside them in their moments of uncertainty and insecurity—not criticizing, but consoling and reassuring him. In all this, we must remember they are not perfect and neither are we. Sometimes we forget this and try to mother our men.

It is essential that we allow our men to stand as kings and warriors, even if their stands are macho and irrational. It is easy to feel that they don't have a clue about or the slightest idea what they are doing and we want to take over and do it ourselves. That is how we end up overwhelmed and frustrated. Give them some breathing space. God guides them just as He guides us.

Lighten Up. Stop trying to control and orchestrate every area of your husband's life. If you want to lose him emotionally just keep being possessive and domineering! Men need space, but, most of all, they need our confidence.

Oh, one final note. Remember, *he's not yours.* Your husband belongs to God. No matter what shape he's in. Don't fight his vision. Don't resent its place in his life; flow with it. Become an intricate part of the vision. Fuel the fire and help make it happen.

CHAPTER SEVEN

MANAGING A MARRIAGE MISTAKE

All marriages are not mistakes simply because the involved parties deem them to be so. Although we may have entered into holy matrimony with misconceptions, preconceived notions, and unrealistic expectations that have left us disappointed, frustrated, and often, seeking divorce as a resolution, we may well have all of the ingredients needed for a healthy marriage.

Although there may be years of damage to undo for some of us, certain principles apply overall that may be helpful in managing as you embark on the healing of your marriage.

First, We Must Correct Our Wrong Thinking. It doesn't matter how we got off track or who led us there, so let's not look in our past for someone to blame. We should now look at our situations and define specifically the problems. Defining the prob-

parents were like mine, they did not have knock-down, drag-out fights in front of the children. I really thought that everything was fine because our home was safe, stable, and secure, and my parents were consistently loving and reassuring toward us. What I didn't know was that their bedroom was just short of Armageddon, for they settled their differences there. What I also didn't know was that my mother was going through hell with my father, but because she cared more about our welfare than her own romantic ideals, she maintained a wholesome posture before the children.

You did not marry your daddy. Don't expect your husband to be a carbon copy of him. Don't expect him to be a reasonable facsimile. Don't expect him to even remotely possess the characteristics of your father. There will never be anyone like your dad. Grow up. On the other hand, for some of us who did not grow up as daddy's little girl, this is good news. However, it is not fair to our husbands to transfer our anger and disdain for our fathers to them. Even though we may see some of the same behavior, we must come into the marriage with an open mind and a willingness to accept our mate for who he is. The biggest mistake that many of us make when making a marriage decision is to either ignore warning signals of trouble or to think that we will be able to change the other person. When you see distasteful behavior or an issue of concern, you must deal with that behavior or concern. It will only magnify after marriage. If you are disgusted by his eating habits now, they will become a sore spot and a source of conflict in the marriage later. If you are uncomfortable with his flirtatious behavior now, you will surely be more uncomfortable after you say "I do."

I truly hope you did not enter your marriage believing that love would pay the bills. I am amazed when women marry men who have never worked for more than a few months at a time, believing that the marriage will make them responsible. If this were the case with you, don't allow yourself to be fixated in the past. A woman's got to do what a woman's got to do. You may need to become financially resourceful until times get better.

Be Thou Made Whole. By now, I pray, that an earnest assessment of your situation has led you to know that it's time to put this book down and go to the altar. That it's time to seek God to correct your thinking. It's time to rededicate your life and to seek restoration and renewal from the God who heals His people. It's time to look to the source of your strength and yes, maybe it's time to repent. Repent, for surely we have not been all that we have needed to be. Before you can reestablish your relationship with your husband, you must establish a strong prayer life with God. Only a relationship with Christ is going to pull you through. I am a witness that a walk with God is what determines the success or failure of a marriage.

Make Up Your Mind. Most of the turmoil experienced when we find ourselves in an uncomfortable marriage is the mixed feelings that we may be having concerning its resolution. Shall I leave or shall I stay? Maybe he will change. What about the children? What about the house? If I leave him, will he ever get straightened out? Make a decision and be prepared to suffer the consequences. Only you can determine what's best, based on the Word of God. Ask yourself, "Is my marriage salvageable and am I willing to pay the price to keep it?" If your answer is yes, know that you should be prepared to do spiritual battle to save it. For it is the device of the devil to destroy marriage because in so doing, he destroys the community and weakens the effect of the local church.

Remember, you have a critical role in your husband's life. You are aiding God in building him up. If Satan can tear you away from that task, he has not only succeeded in separating your family but also in hindering the work and ministry that God has for you and your husband which, needless to say, will affect the lives of thousands and is the purpose for your existence.

When we understand that it's not about us and can see the whole picture, we realize who the enemy is. If you want your marriage, you must fight for it. The fight will not be easy, but saving your marriage will be well worth it.

Let God Fight Your Battles. We must be careful not to "lay our religion down" as we face unpleasant issues and situations in our marriage. There may be times when you will need the strength simply to keep your mouth closed. For some of us, keeping our mouths closed is easier said then done. I began my marriage as a yeller and screamer. When things didn't suit me I went OFF! The Holy Spirit convicted me about my behavior and I began to seek the Lord for the ability to keep my mouth closed when I became angry with Bob. The results were incredible. They were down right rewarding. My husband was thrown for such a loop by my silence during a confrontation that would have normally blown the roof off of the house that he showered me with gifts for days because he felt like such a jerk. I LOVE IT! Nothing we can do or say will be as effective as the Holy Spirit moving on the heart of man.

When we realize that Satan is the culprit who is trying to destroy our relationship with our husbands, we can be healed and extend forgiveness to them. That being the case, we must petition God to renew the passion that we once had for our husbands. If the bond of intimacy can be broken between us, we are fighting a losing battle. Sometimes the comfort of loving arms aids us in enduring the heat of the battle.

Those of us who have found our husbands in adultery must look pass our humiliation and other emotions and accept the fact that this is a sin issue. If we can be big girls and subsequently mighty warriors for God, we cannot only win our husbands but the soul of the women they are seeing. Now wouldn't that make Satan mad.

Do Not Compare Your Marriage To Anyone Else's. Sometimes we have friends and family members who attempt to show us that we are missing something in our relationship with our spouses or that they are shortchanging us in some way. This situation has caused more break ups than anything.

Each marriage is unique. The things that some would say are bad aspects of your marriage are merely characteristics of you and your spouse. In other words, that's what makes you different and special. When we buy leather, suede, or silk garments, the manufacturer usually attaches a note telling us that the variations in the material are not flaws but are characteristic of that fabric. The same applies to your marriage.

If your spouse is honoring your marriage, don't allow anyone to dictate what is right or wrong for the two of you. Some little, old lady will always be telling you how she managed to stay with her husband for 150 years without a moment's trouble. Chances are she's in denial, on drugs or just plum forgot!

If your spouse releases you to have a career, don't let some frustrated homebody tell you that you should be home wiping peanut butter and jelly off the walls. Similarly, if your husband desires you to stay home and is providing for your family, don't feel inadequate because you're not an overworked, unappreciated working girl. On the other hand, if he wants you to stay home and he's not providing for the family, that matter is between you, him and God. Keep your mother out of your decision making. You're her baby and she will respond emotionally to the situation rather than with Godly counsel.

If you feel that your marriage was a mistake, be sure that the conclusion is yours. Only you and your husband can set the standards of happiness and success for your lives, and the two of you should not base those standards on social dictates and expectations.

Before we go further, I would like to reiterate a statement. The role of the husband is to provide for and to protect the wife and children. That statement brings us to my next point.

Keep Him In His Place! Unfortunately, most men interpret being the head of the family to mean that they are the official "bully" of the home because no one has taught them, or they refuse to accept that with authority comes responsibility and accountability; both for which they will answer to God. The man's place is so very demanding and no doubt sometimes quite overwhelming. That is why it is important that we resign ourselves to keeping him there. For if he doesn't stay in his place, we are forced out of ours.

Some men like to beat their chest and remind you of who wears the pants in the home. However, when it comes time for action, they are all too willing to relinquish authority and to say "You do it." Therefore, to reinforce the principle of authority with responsibility, it may be necessary to encourage your husband frequently to be the decision maker for your family. This should also entail his initiating any necessary actions related to his decisions unless he asks for your assistance. As said before, we may be the one who speaks the vision, but it is important to remember, the next step is his.

Yes I know it could mean waiting for our Lord to return! Don't forget there are positive ways to motivate our spouses without being nags. We have the power of influence, a tool that God has given us, not just to get what we want but to aid Him in the molding of our husbands' lives. Remember, our roles as wives are to work with God as He builds up or brings our husbands into the fullness of their potential.

Keeping him in his place does not apply exclusively to financial issues. There are other areas of the marriage where we should allow our husband to have a free hand. Often we try to set the guidelines for their relationship with the children. They are the fathers. Fathers can't be mothers; mothers can't be fathers. Generally speaking, fathers break rules, they don't enforce them. The relationship between father and child is more recreational. The relationship between mother and child is custodial and structured.

As a daddy's girl, I adored my father, causing my mother much frustration in my early years for she was making all the sacrifices and caring for me, but daddy was the object of my affection. Now that I am a mother, I realize how wonderful she was and our relationship has blossomed into a cherished friendship. Don't worry. The children may see you as the "Wicked Witch of the West" right now, but if they live long enough they'll know the real deal.

Not only should we avoid touching their relationship with our children, but we must allow them the freedom to express themselves. Heaven help you if you're married to a slob. Sometimes we must decide whether we want our house to be a comfortable home for everyone or a "show room." It is painfully true that a man's home is his castle and as long as he's paying the mortgage, he can leave his socks where he wants. Ugh! In other words, we may want our homes to be neat but when it's a major area of conflict, find less disruptive ways to resolve the issue than nagging and complaining. I have found it interesting that some of us can make a mess and it's okay; however, as soon as our husbands leave one thing out of place we go bonkers!

Bearing this in mind, we must lighten up. For a man to maintain the confidence and the integrity within himself that is crucial to his being the head of the woman and the priest of his home, he must clearly know and be who he is. If we help him in these areas, he will stay in his place.

Love Him For Who He Is. Do not expect to have a strong marriage if you try to change your husband into something he is not. I am constantly approached by women who are disheartened with their marriages because their husbands are not like their former lovers or the man of their dreams. Sometimes I think we lose sight on what is really important. For these same women will tell me their husbands are nice guys who are financially responsible and loving fathers, but. ...." When we thank and praise God for the good we have in our husbands, He will move on our behalves to take care of the other concerns.

Do What You Can To Make Things Better. For example, if you have financial problems, sit down together and determine what the problem is. It's not always the lack of money. Sometimes, financial difficulties are a result of poor money management. Determine who is best qualified to handle the books and turn them over to that person. If there is a substance abuse or gambling problem, deal with it realistically. Remember, sometimes it's not that we have a financial problem; it may be that we have husband problems. Face that fact if necessary and seek counseling.

If your husband is having an affair, find out if you are contributing to it. And you may be. You would be astonished at the number of women who come to me because their husbands are cheating. After a short conversation, I can ascertain that they have not been dutiful in the marriage bed for months--and even years. Uh dah!

Some of us have let our appearance go and have not taken time to pamper ourselves and to make ourselves desirable to our husbands. You may not have noticed but there are tons of gorgeous women in this world who would love to get their hands on your husband. Give them a run for their money. Be not deceived, there is always someone after your husband. Whether she's bold enough to call your house or just lurks in the shadows waiting for you to mess up, she's there.

Be mindful that being attractive does not mean looking like a fluzzie. Some of us can go to the extreme in this area. Please, ladies, no plunging necklines, deep splits, tight skirts and slacks, or tacky panty lines. Modest apparel with tasteful accessories works wonders.

Believe me, love begets love. Although we all love to receive attention and affection, a time comes in our marriages when we must be willing to give the same without coercion. I understand that women feel rejected when their husbands don't initiate romance. I know as well that tradition says to wait coyly until the man makes the first move, but honey, he is yours. Go after him. Seduce him in the middle of the day if you care to. Be adventurous and unpredictable. Add excitement to his life. Sometimes men are simply looking for a change in routine or some variety.

If there is a problem with the children, it must be straightened out. Some things will not be resolved overnight. Some things can be. If we keep in mind that we are to cleave to our husbands and remember that the children do not come first, we are off to a good start. Get your children on a schedule that will allow you time with your husband, and for goodness' sake, keep them out of your bed.

Clean your house. Men hate a dirty house. They know that you are busy and may themselves be the biggest slobs in town. A friend who runs a cleaning business shared with me that Christian women have the filthiest houses of all she has seen. That's not good, my sisters. I have talked to men who have told me that the condition of their households has deterred them from interacting with their families and even venturing to do some positive things in the home, for they see it as a waste of time and a hopeless case.

Stay home sometimes. Some of us spend too much time out of the home, either socializing or going to church too much, and leave our mates and children to fend for themselves. This does not please God. We are ever learning, but never coming to the knowledge of the truth, for Paul encouraged us to stay single if possible because the single woman is free to go for God. However, he says, the married woman must first attend to the matters of her husband (I Corinthians, chapter seven). Your husband may just need some attention, particularly if he is not a believer. We could go on and on in naming typical situations that stress our marriages, but I believe you get the picture. Do what you can and trust God to go beyond your human abilities.

Thou Shalt Not Commit Adultery. You would

be astonished by the number of women who have used the troubles in their marriages to justify having affairs. The most certain way to become entangled in adultery is to have a man as your confidant. You may not feel attracted to him initially, but after a while his consoling you, understanding of your needs, and ministering to you will make him attractive. Before you know it you will be in his arms and in his bed. Remember, even muddy water looks good to someone dying of thirst on the desert. If you are frustrated enough, Gomer Pyle will look enticing.

You must also beware of the lesbian spirit. For it seeks broken and vulnerable women to prey on. The lesbian offers the security, protection, and comfort lacking from a man and slowly but surely weaves a web so tight that only God Himself will be able to free you from it. It may not become a sexual issue, but the emotional bondage is profound.

At either rate, we cannot concentrate on restoring our marriage when another man is in our heart. It is wrong. It is adultery. If you are not sleeping with him but yearn for him in your heart, it's still adultery. There is no justification, there is no excuse, there is no Godly solution for the relationship except to give him up!

Redirect Your Focus. We all know that God can deliver us out of a situation. However, sometimes He will deliver us in a situation. This means that the circumstances may never change but He changes us in our perspective and responses, so we can grow and thrive in Him through our obedience regardless of what surrounds us.

If you are a woman who is trapped in a situation that has existed for years and for what ever reason you can see no way out and no hope of change, my word to you is to find a cleft in the rock. In Psalms 18 David proclaims God to be his rock. We are not talking about a stone or the type of rocks that we use to landscape our yards. We are talking about boulders. The rocks of Palestine were structures which were large enough to conceal a man and protect him from his predators. These rocks have clefts or nooks and crannies that one can slip into and be hidden from the enemy.

Sometimes in our marriages, we have to find a safe place, a place of fulfillment where we can rest and redirect our focus. In other words, get a life! Move onto some other things. Pursue interests that may have been pushed aside or unrealized for whatever the reason. Our romantic circumstances should not deter us from having a rich and full life. This could mean finishing our education, changing careers, starting a career, focusing on the children or the grandchildren, traveling, redecorating the house, or any number of things. The point is to stop looking around and start looking up.

Trust In The Lord. In Psalms 121, David made a firm decision. He said, "I will lift up mine eyes unto the hills, from whence cometh my help. My help cometh from the Lord, which made heaven and earth." When we come to grips with the fact that our husbands are not the source of our existence or sub-stance, we can dispose of our fears of their rejection and go on with our lives. We, like David, must raise our thinking above the mole hills of problems in our lives and look toward the mountain Himself and discover that compared to Him our circumstances are but a small thing. In so doing, we can manage our marriage mistakes and may, indeed, realize that our marriage was not a mistake after all.

GOD SPEAKS TO WOMEN

Stephanie McAlister Jennings

ORDER BLANK

☐ Please send me ___ copy (ies) of GOD SPEAKS TO WOMEN at $10.00 each, (plus $2.50 shipping and handling.).

☐ I am not ordering at this time, but please add me to your mailing list.

Name_____

Address _____

City_____State____Zip Code_____

Home Telephone_____

Subtotal_____

Shipping and Handling_____

Taxes_____

Total_____

(Maryland resident add 5% sales tax)

Send check or money order, made payable to:
SMJ
Stephanie Jennings Ministries
12512 Kingsview
Mitchellville, MD 20721
301-390-0328